To Char

THE LONG RIDE HOME

Peace and joy!

A Journey through Grief to Peace and Happiness

Jeannie Vansickle

Jeannie Vansickle

BALBOA
PRESS
A DIVISION OF HAY HOUSE

ISBN: 978-1-4525-6266-7 (sc)
ISBN: 978-1-4525-6267-4 (e)
ISBN: 978-1-4525-6268-1 (hc)
Library of Congress Control Number: 2012921258

Balboa Press books may be ordered through booksellers or by contacting:

Balboa Press
A Division of Hay House
1663 Liberty Drive
Bloomington, IN 47403
www.balboapress.com
1-(877) 407-4847

Printed in the United States of America

Balboa Press rev. date: 11/28/2012

Author's Note

As a former English major and unofficial head of the office grammar police, I feel the need to provide the following disclaimer:

I acknowledge there are errors in punctuation and grammar in this manuscript. Much of the material was taken directly from my journals exactly as I wrote it, often through tears and without ever thinking it would be seen by anyone else. In writing this book, I decided not to make correction or changes, but rather present the entries as I had written them in the moment.

To Larry

(1941-2007)

Everything I am
is because you loved me.

FORWARD

MY STORY

I wonder why anyone would want to read my story. Joan Didion already wrote the story of losing her husband in an instant. So did Anne Roiphe in Epilogue after her husband's sudden death and Aurora Winter wrote from Heartbreak to Happiness. So many books have been written about losing the love of one's life, why is my story any different?

Maybe because….it's my story.

I have read many, many grief books and continue to read more. Maybe someone will read mine and find something in it that resonates just for them. And maybe in the process, I will finally be at peace and figure out what I am supposed to do with this life I am left to live. Right now I have not a clue.

Nearly three years have passed since that late night when the doorbell roused me from my sleep and my life as I knew it for 40 years began spirally out of control. A friend was coming to take me to an emergency room 90 miles away where my husband lay hooked up to a ventilator. Dying before my eyes. I'm not sure I can find the words to express what transpired and how it has impacted my formerly happy life and my then sense of well-being. That is gone for me forever, I fear.

The following night he passed away, leaving me forever. The waiting room had been filled with friends and family for all the hours of vigilance. I chose to drive his car back home alone. During that hour and half ride, I screamed, I wailed, I cursed him and planned his celebration of life. All the time---How could this be happening to me? How will I ever live without him?

****

I wrote the piece above over two years ago. Once I was able to surrender to truth of Larry's death, I was able to savor the memories we made together and begin the climb out of the hole in my heart to find peace and happiness.

I think I am finally there and this is my story. I thought I couldn't live without him and now I know I can.

PROLOGUE

January 17

You were leaving for your conference in Peoria. I was in the bathroom putting on my face, when you came in and said, "I'm heading out now" and gave me a kiss. I remember that I said, "Get back here, that wasn't good enough". I'm so thankful that I called you back for that second kiss. Little did I know it would be our last.

Premonition....that afternoon

It was an icy, cold winter day. On my way home from the office, I stopped to check on a vacant house I had listed. Upon entering the house I was gripped with a sudden overwhelming fear. I locked the door behind me, turned on all the lights and rushed through the house and back to my car filled with terror. It was just turning dark and I have never been so terrified in my life. That is not like me; I'm not afraid of the dark or spirits lurking in the shadows. I drove in a panic to the safety of our home. This all took place between 5 and 6p.m. Was your body already shutting down as I was shaking in terror?

Was it a forewarning of what was to come?

Life Interrupted

The Doorbell Rang at Ten

Later that evening after a bowl of soup and a glass of wine, I was relaxed and calm again.

Then the doorbell rang and my life began the downward spiral. The doorbell was ringing frantically and then there was pounding on the door. Finally our friend shouted, "It's me, Steve, open up…it's about Larry." I was gripped by that fear again. He connected me to a Dr. in the emergency room at St. Francis hospital. The doctor's words, "You need to get here now" made no sense. It was ten o'clock at night and I was 90 miles away. My lame response was "But what do you mean?" "Get here now", he repeated. Steve had to tell me to put shoes on! My heart was pounding and my head was spinning.

We drove 100 miles an hour to Peoria. When we arrived at the ER, I learned Larry was now in Intensive Care on a ventilator. He would never have wanted that and I wouldn't have allowed it. I kissed him, stroked his cheek, and held his hand and he wasn't there. I yelled at him---"Snap out of it!" "Damnit, wake up!" In my heart of hearts, I knew he was gone from me.

The little waiting room outside Intensive Care was filled to overflowing with people who loved him. They drove there for us and to hold vigil with me.

I kissed him goodnight late on Thursday, January 18th and went to the hotel to get some sleep. I had decided to have the machines shut off the next day at noon. He slipped away during the night and was gone from me forever. I didn't go back to the hospital to see him again…I couldn't bear to see my Larry hooked up to all those machines again.

The following week we held a Celebration of Life for him at his favorite restaurant. Over 300 people were there. Friends produced a DVD, a brochure and found the perfect poem for him. He was there with us while we laughed and cried and toasted him. And, I know he loved it!!

I'm Right Here

I've only slipped away into the next room
    with scotch in hand.
I am I, and you are you,
Whatever we were to each other, we are still.
Call me by my old familiar name.
Speak of me in the easy manner which you always used.
Put no difference in your tone.
Wear no forced air of solemnity or sorrow.
Laugh as we always laughed
At the jokes we shared together.
Play, smile, and think of me.
Let my name be ever the household word
    that it always was.
Let it be spoken without an effort
Without the ghost of a shadow upon it.
Life means all it has ever meant.
It is the same as it always was.
Why should I be out of mind because
    I am out of sight?
I am but waiting for you.
Somewhere very near,
Just around the corner.
All is well. Love, Larry

Day 18

How have I made it this far??

I'm amazed at how much the cards and letters have meant to me. I look forward to the mail every day—so many cards. I pour a glass of wine and relish the words of praise about my dear Larry. I still can't believe this is real. How can this be happening?

Day 42

I'm so scared. I don't want to have a life without Larry. Our life together was so easy, so comfortable. 40 years of being together and sharing our love. I'm filled with fear.

I Did Not Die

Do not stand by grave and weep;
I am not there, I do not sleep.
I am a thousand winds that blow.
I am the diamond glints on the snow.
I am the sunlight on ripened grain.
I am the gentle autumn rain.

When you waken in the morning's hush,
I am the swift uplifting rush
Of quiet birds in circled flight.
I am the soft stars that shine at night.
Do not stand at my grave and cry;
I am not there, I am everywhere.

(A Hopi Prayer)

And I go on............

Business as usual: showing houses, listing houses, writing contracts, attending meetings—but, it's not as usual. Tears well up, my heart cries out. There's a burning, churning inside and I can't wait to get back home where I can wail and sob, alone with my broken heart and shattered dreams.

I even went to my real estate convention in Las Vegas, as if I really gave a damn!

Better than staying home alone....I guess.

I just want my life back!!!!

March

Today I decided to change my journaling into letters to Larry.

My dear, sweet Larry, I'm writing to you.

I always want to call you to tell you some little thing. We used to call each other several times a day. Now you never call me! And, I have no recording of your voice. That wonderful voice that could have been on radio. I so want to hear your voice again. How about in a dream—please!

Oh, thanks for helping me open that jar of my prescription cream last night. I could not open it; I could hardly get my hand around the large lid. I banged it on the counter several times—it wouldn't budge. In my frustration, I cried out, "Larry, help me open this jar!" And you did! It opened on the next try—thanks!

Easter morning

I hate you! I hate you! You bastard, you son of a bitch! How could you do this to me?
I am crying so hard I can hardly see. My heart is broken—thanks to you! Damn you!

That Night

Yesterday I sold your car. When the nice young man who purchased your car handed me your license plates, it felt like the moment when the dead soldier's wife is handed the folded flag. It was devastating. That car was such a part of you. It was your brand and you were so proud of it. Seeing that car as the garage door slowly opened always meant, Larry's home! And now, seeing that car each time was a cruel reminder that you were gone. It was a punch in the stomach every time I came home. It was more than I could bear.
So, I hope you can understand why I wrote those curses. I love you so much and miss you terribly. My life will never be the same. Will I ever be happy again?

****

Well, I can't stop crying. I've felt like it all day and now it's here. I'm watching "As Time Goes By" on PBS—remembering how we used to so enjoy watching it together.
You loved Lionel's cryptic outlook on life. Much like yours. We had such a good time together. We were so good------!!

A few days later

I've been a little happier these past few days because I learned that you are o.k. "over there". My cousin Lois has communicated with a medium friend of hers who has had some sort of contact with you. The first thing he told her was that you were "mad as hell that you had passed over." That's how I knew for sure it was you!! He told her that you had met up with someone that you knew and had become close to that person---Bob or Marc??? I hope so.

****

The latest grief book I'm reading says to list the losses, as in:
I lost my lover,
my best friend,
and my chef,
my caretaker,
my errand runner,
my travel companion,
my weekend buddy,
my dinner partner,
my cottage lover,
the best cuddler,
the one I was planning my life with.
Oh so very, very much I have lost!

Later that week

I lifted the container holding your ashes—it was heavy. I opened the lid and saw bone fragments!! It creeped me out. Later I tried to throw up—but I couldn't. I didn't put my finger down my throat or anything like that, but I felt like wretching. I just didn't think the ashes would be heavy. You probably knew that—you knew everything.

****

Last night I slept on your side of the bed hoping I would dream about you. It didn't work.

****

Listen to this: The window was open and I had just drifted off to sleep. I heard a bird, two cries and that was all. It startled me out my sleep and somehow I thought it was you. And, it sounded so sad and maybe hurting. Are you o.k.? Are you struggling to get to the other side or trying to communicate with me? It was alarming! Do we have ravens around here? Will you be more settled once we scatter your ashes?

I'm going to put some ashes under the tree we are planting for you on Saturday, I hope that's o.k. That will be a permanent place for you to rest. The remainder will travel the world. We will send them out to sea at the cottage and when I release them into Kentucky Lake, they will head to the Gulf of Mexico. You will be everywhere—just like your poem!

Day after the tree planting

I played golf today with Tom and Joan. You were there with us. I hit a beautiful long straight drive over the water on #8. I couldn't believe it! Tom and I both said Larry hit that ball for me. Thanks! I also had about a 30 foot putt, but I knew you didn't do that for me—you weren't a great putter. Ha!

Oh, I forgot to tell you that I carried your ashes to the tree planting in a Chivas Regal tin. Everyone thought that was most appropriate. So many of our friends were there for the ceremony. Lori and Reese read poems they had written for you. I was proud to be your wife----I hate the word widow!

Widow Not!!

Widow, widow
How I hate that word.
I'm not, I'm not!
I'm a woman who lost her husband,
The love of her life.
My heart is broken and filled with pain.
I'm not wearing black,
Not wailing at the graveside,
Not locked in my room.
I'm just a woman who lost her husband.
Widow not!!!

May

One of things I've noticed since you've gone is how little patience I have.
And you know how little I had before!! I think it's because I'm still so angry (at you!) and, of course, scared. Will I ever be o.k. again? I'm so scared about my finances---will I end up a bag lady!??

You did know that I loved you with every part of my being—even when I was mad at you? I still love you with all my heart. I always knew how much you loved me, did you know how much I loved you. Did I love you enough?

I will always treasure a note I received from my cousin, Jeri, right after you died. We had all been together just weeks before you left us, sitting out on the porch at the inn on Cape Cod drinking wine. I was, I imagine, pontificating about something and you turned to her and said "God help me, I love that woman." I know you did and that comforts me every day.

****

I remember the feel
of your body encircling mine.
Your sweet lips caressing,
Your blue eyes adoring
and it makes me smile.
And then I cry.

May 3

Margie and I are on the way to Connecticut for Kate's graduation. Our niece ,who you adored and who adored you, is graduating with her Master's from UCONN this weekend. You would be so proud! You will be missed and I will go to our cottage for the first time without you.
You never got to see the new roof!

May 5, 2007 Graduation Day

After the long, boring ceremony we went to dinner. The table had one extra place setting, we left it for you. Russ ordered a scotch on rocks, the waiter delivered to the empty place setting and we all had a drink from it. You are so loved and so missed!
Even when I am so pissed----you are so loved by me.

Two days later---Voices

I was sitting on the deck at Russ's and suddenly I heard my name. I thought it was you…"Hey, Jeannie", just as clear as a bell. I heard it several times and called Laurie outside, she heard it too. It turned out to be a Black-capped Chickadee. Well, I heard what I heard! I'm waiting for you to show up in our backyard.

Interesting note: "Birds can be symbols of freedom to the deceased, a way to let the living know they're souring in the sky and not in the ground or in an urn. Birds are a sign of life and an expanded consciousness. Birds look down on us and it's not so different than angel spirits." *Allison DuBois* I love this!!

Firsts without you since you've gone!

First time in Connecticut
First time to see my Dad
First time at the cottage
First time at Russ and Laurie's
First time I heard you call my name.

Home Again

I walked to your tree this morning. I sat and stared at the place where I had left some of your ashes. I shed a few tears and cursed a few curses---damn you anyway!
I brought home some leaves from your tree. Maybe for an art piece.

The Tree

Today I walked to your tree
just to see
if maybe, just maybe
you might be there.
Alas, it was not so.
You are not there.
You are gone
from me
forever.
And I will love you
always and forever.

Later that month

I've just returned from the real estate conference in D.C. When I'm away it seems less real. Then I get home and it's back to reality—you are gone!! I'm alone and I'm scared! How am I going to make it without you for the next 20 years (or more)??

I can't stop crying and you're not here to hold me. There is a constant gnawing in my stomach and all day—all the time—I'm on the verge of tears. I feel like I'm walking on a tightrope and any moment I could fall into the abyss. I can't concentrate, I can't complete tasks, I'm distracted, can't focus, don't pay bills, papers are scattered all over the house, disorganized, not interested in cooking, even gardening doesn't excite me.

I looked out on our deck this morning and saw all the evenings when we lit the torches, started a fire in the firepit. Just the two of us out there with our drinks and our dreams. Thanks for ruining my life!!

****

Three days later

Another first! I grilled tonight! A flank steak and it turned out great! Ha! I can grill without you!

Later watched your DVD and cried all way through it.

****

Memorial Day

First time I entertained without you. The party was a success, but it just didn't seem right without you. Marian thanked me for having the party and giving her a chance to be here (at our house) without you. It will take a lot of getting used to. Tom cooked on your grill and enjoyed your single malt scotch. Another first for all of us.

****

Baby steps......
"Baby steps count, as long as you go forward." *Chris Gardner*

****

My Vanity Suffers Without You

You are missing out on seeing cute little me. Lately people have been telling me how cute I look. One insensitive acquaintance told me I looked good for someone in mourning!

I seem to spend an inordinate amount of time creating myself each morning. To what purpose?? You aren't here to tell me how good I look.

Every morning I would come downstairs, you would be on the phone and I would prance in front of you. You would give that approving smile and a thumbs up. Occassionally you would give me a look that said "try again".

Now I try so hard to look good. I guess so that everyone will think I feel good too. Just this morning I tried on three different tops, two jackets, and a dozen different jewelry combinations. Not to mention the shoes!

And, after all that effort, I'm not sure I liked the results. You weren't here to give me your comments. So often, you said, "Sharp outfit" or just "Wow". Best of all I loved the smiling thumbs up you frequently gave me. What a great start to my day. I thank you for that---always!

June 24th---Ashes at the Cottage

Happy anniversary! I woke up crying this morning. You are supposed to be here with me. My heart is broken.

You are calling to me as I write. The Black-capped Chickadee is sitting on the power line just outside and I can hear you clear as a bell: "Hey, Jeannie, Hey, Jeannie"

You are here on this special day. Thank you for coming.

Oh, I forgot to tell you Russ left some of your ashes at the Italian American Club near the horseshoe court. You really are everywhere!!!

It's a beautiful day, cool and breezy. A perfect day at the cottage for sending your ashes out to sea. Kate went down to the beach this morning. She said, "Larry would want me to relax."

****

I was just thinking that this bird thing began awhile ago. Just a few weeks after you were gone, Donna came to spend the night. In the morning when we got up, we saw a robin sitting in the tree right outside our front door. It was February! Donna said it was you! Maybe she was right….you keep stopping by. Thanks!

Later that night.........

I wonder what you thought about today. Lots of friends and family were here to honor you. Russ spoke about you. He said you were "a ladies' man, a man's man, a kind man, and most of all a wise man". So true. We stood at the bank of the salt marshes as the tide was going out. I tossed your ashes into the water, then we all threw white rose petals and cried as they floated out to sea. Laurie read "I'm Right Here"and the Hopi Prayer. Then Russ opened the Famous Grouse (your favorite scotch). Kate said "it's 5 o'clock somewhere" and we all had a toast.

Another bittersweet moment; another special memory created on what would have been our 40th anniversary.

Next morning

I picked up your picture, as I often do. Sometimes, I kiss it, sometimes I just hold it close and sometimes I slap it. Just as I touched the photo, I heard it—"Hey, Jeannie". Nice way to start the morning. You keep stopping by!

The big problem for me right now is figuring out where I belong. Here at the cottage where I feel most at peace? This was our special place. All my dear friends are in Champaign. My wonderful little family is here. OR, should I just go somewhere and start over? I don't know what to do with the rest of my life now that it is not what I had planned. And, what about money?? Any ideas??

Two days later....

I worry sometimes that I didn't love you enough. I mean that I didn't let you know enough how much I loved you. Just how much our life together meant to me. I'm sorry for all the times I snapped at you. Was I not compassionate enough when your father died, when your Grandma died, when you had cancer? I was trying to be brave for you. Maybe you thought I was uncaring or cold. Please say no! You were/are the best thing that ever happened to me.

****

I wondered what to do with the attractive red canister that had contained your ashes. Russ said to leave it and he might make a lamp out of it. He always manages to make me smile.

July 4th

I just thought about your ashes floating away and let out a huge sob. Sometimes when I'm eating I think of you, I gag and I can't swallow. But, not to worry, it hasn't stopped me from eating. Some women lose weight when they lose their husbands—not me! I can't even get that little perk out of all this! Damn!

A few days later…

Can you believe even grocery shopping can make me cry? Today walking through the aisles, shopping for one, had me on the verge of tears. We had such fun and camaraderie planning and preparing meals. So many food memories. I looked at the country ribs and nearly burst into tears. How did you make that marinade?

Brussel sprouts make me cry.
You loved them, I hated them.
I bought them for you
Because I loved you.

The Farmer's Market makes me cry.
Tomatoes are there, bright red and ripe.
I bought them for you because
You loved them and I loved you.

A recipe for stir-fried lima beans
Brings me to tears.
I prepared those beans for you.
You loved them and I loved you.

****

I wish this were a soap opera. Then there would
be a chance you would come back from
the dead.

****

August

Tonight I lost it when I got home. Maybe it was being at dinner with all the couples.
I cried, I screamed and yelled, pounded the counter, and punched the leather couch.
I so wanted to throw a glass against the wall and watch it shatter. Shatter as my life is shattered.

I decided to sleep in your closet with your shirt as my pillow so I could be close to you. (The floor is very hard.)

LESSONS LEARNED.......so far

The car wash is a great place to cry and scream!

Don't bang my head on the shower wall---it's ceramic tile. Ouch!!

Sleeping on your side of the bed didn't bring you to me in a dream.

Throwing cookie sheets and cake pans is great for venting pain and anger---they make lots of noise and don't break!

I'm out of scotch. I'll have to buy my own now. You always made sure there was Chivas here for me. Can I even afford Chivas now???

Sometimes, I just need to stop and breathe. Then I can go on. Breathe, just breathe.....

September 14th----Your birthday

We gathered at your tree to release balloons and we sang Happy Birthday. I know you would have hated that part—well, too bad! We wrote messages on the balloons and released them to the brilliant, cloudless sky. We watched as they floated away, all different colors— the silver one reflecting the sunlight. A spectacular sight. Then back to our house for Bloody Marys and a toast to you. We have such great friends and how lucky I am that they are all here for me.

I had a birthday card for you too, but it wouldn't fly. The verse was just perfect.
"Now and forever, come what may, just as you are….**I will love you.**"

Later that week....

I made chicken soup, it was very therapeutic. I felt like you were with me.

And, oh, I knew you with me in the shower this morning—you touched my butt!!

****

Tonight it hit me---fall is coming. Cold mornings and cool windy evenings. I always loved this time of year. It meant sitting by the fireplace with a nightcap, cuddling in bed and a renewed closeness. And, now you're gone!

Ashes at the Lake

Wow! What an event. The weather was perfect, a gem of a day. Bette made wonderful preparations—your Commodore photo was set up on an easel beside a dozen red roses.

We had hors d'oeuvres and plenty to drink. We cruised around the lake for awhile before stopping at sunset. We toasted you with the scotch that Ken brought for the occasion.

Nancy poured hers overboard and said "Here's to you, Larry." I read the Hopi Prayer and poured the ashes into the lake. Everyone tossed the roses to float away with your ashes. What a wonderful group of friends we have here.

The next morning everyone came up to the condo for Bloody Marys then breakfast at the Yacht Club. It was great to be with all our boating friends again. We have so many memories of our boating days. Bill and Bette made this a really special occasion for me and you too!

****

Long drive home. Russ called to tell me Dad is in the hospital again with pneumonia.

You Came to Me Last Night

I saw you walking on the dock,
I called your name.
You came to me and we kissed.
You looked so real…
How deceiving.
A ghost of your old self, you held me
in your weightless arms.
It made me glad to see you,
Now you are gone, again….
     I cry new tears.

Things that Make Me Think of You:

The new WWII series on PPS
The western just out—"310 to Yuma"—you would have seen it by now
Bloody Marys, of course
A menu of single malt scotches
The S&K ad that just came in the mail offering two suits for the price of one.
Whenever I see lamb on the menu
Your clothes,
your scent--Givenchy Gentleman,
your pictures,
your books,
your wall of awards,
the gold finches you fed
and our backyard that we created together!

October

Just talked to Russ. My Dad is not doing well.

A few days later....

Marge called to tell me Dad is in the hospital in isolation with a staff infection.
It doesn't look good right now.

I could lose both of you in the same year.

****

It's 5:30 am and I've been up an hour already. This would be the time you would come wandering downstairs to join me for coffee. Where the hell are you?? I want you here!!

****

Well, I did it!! I paid off all the credit cards <u>and</u> my car! Never in my adult life have I not had a car payment! I'd still rather be up to my ears in debt <u>with</u> you!!
Oh my! I was in your closet again---I just can't get rid of your clothes.

****

Marilyn stopped by for a glass of wine. She talked about how lucky I was to have had the time we had together and how much we loved each other. I know I am fortunate for that, but I wasn't ready to say goodbye!

We also talked about the fabric art piece she is going to make with material from your shirts and ties. A memory piece!

****

Writing to you is so important to me----even though you don't write back!!

Random Thoughts

Quote from *Maryann*: Death ends a life, but it does not end a relationship. How true!!

****

"Life goes on. I know not why"
$\qquad\qquad$ *Edna St. Vincent Millay*

****

You left me
$\qquad$ left without a word.
I didn't know you were going,
$\qquad$ going away forever.
You were my best friend,
$\qquad$ friends don't leave with no farewell!
No warning whatsoever......
$\qquad$ here today, gone tomorrow.
That really makes me sad and,
$\qquad$ pissed off too!

****

The wound will heal, but the scar will always be there. (From *Dale*)

****

I can't believe this is real. Maybe I'm not strong enough to do this!!

****

I wonder what I should do with this new life that lies ahead. I have no map for this journey. Where am I going and where will I land?

****

I cannot prevent the birds of sorrow from passing over my head. But I can keep them from building a nest.

****

If the eyes had no tears, the soul would have no rainbow.
Native American Proverb

****

GRIEF IS HELL!!!!!!

We Were

There was we.
Now it's me.

We were so good,
just us two.

Happy together
eating, drinking, talking, sharing…
just me and you.

Gone is the we
and now it's just me.

GONE

I wear your blue oxford cloth shirt.
I snuggle with your Peruvian wool sweater.
I sleep in your Taylor Made golf shirt.
And, you're not here.
Not here with me.

I watch the DVD and see
your smile,
your head thrown back in laughter,
your hair blowing in the wind.
And, you're not here.
Not here with me.

I cannot feel your gentle touch.
I cannot smell the cigarettes on your breath.
I cannot kiss your dear sweet lips,
Because you're not here.
You are gone from me
And I am left with tears
and memories.

The Long Ride Home

November

Sitting here crying—I want you back! I want to hold you or better yet have you hold me.
I can't believe this is real. Maybe I'm not really strong enough to do this! I can't stop crying and I am so mad at you! You left me without any warning. I feel like I'm coming unglued. I may start calling people in the middle of the night. Shit!

Can't you just come and sit beside me--------just once!! PLEASE!

All it takes is me just thinking about you never being here again to make the tears flow.
How can this really be true?!

Later in the week

A dream---you were finally there!! We were getting ready to have sex, but we never did because you kept brushing your teeth!!!!!

Another dream: You were holding me in your arms and laughing your big wonderful laugh. Your face was full of love for me. It was that special look you had for me.

Watching "As Time Goes By" again. They were dancing the kitchen. We did that—not often enough. Come dance with me!

Marilyn called today. She is finishing your piece as she refers to it: "Larry's piece".
It's so special. Fabric from your shirts and ties along with photos copied to cloth. Even one of your brass monogrammed buttons from your navy blue blazer. She is also making coin purses for Christmas for Laurie, Kate, Margie and Sara.

Cooking a Larry breakfast this morning. Spicy scrambled eggs, crispy bacon, sautéed potatoes and whole grain toast. I'm crying while I'm cooking, of course.

I keep writing to you and you never reply. Are you alright? Do you miss me too? Are you still watching over me?

I'm keeping a scrapbook of this year. Notes, cards and emails from friends and family, photos of the special events, my poems and those I find that speak to me.

It has been a comforting project to focus on. One of my friends told me she had never heard of such a thing. I do believe she thought it strange. It works for me. I've been reading lots of books on grief and grieving and I often find meaningful passages that I need to write down.

"If you were to live to be one hundred, I would want to live one hundred minus one day, so I'd never have to live a day without you."
Winnie the Pooh

Thanksgiving

This would be the time we'd be planning our trip to Florida for Thanksgiving with Uncle Cliff and Aunt Ella. Jeri and George and Margie are going with me this year. I didn't know what else to do. The two of us have been doing this for the past ten years. I don't know how it will be without you.

Well…we made it. It was a bit like there was an elephant in the room that no one was acknowledging. I kept bringing up your name and no one picked up on it. George had to fill your role as bartender—it was a tough act to follow. Aunt Ella broke down when we said goodbye. First Thanksgiving without you. Next up: Christmas.

****

Chuck and June built shelves in the basement while I was gone. They are amazing—the shelves <u>and</u> Chuck and June.

Oh, my—how much I miss you. I am so concerned that I will forget your laugh, your smile, your voice (that wonderful voice), your touch, your kiss, your chili! The future without you seems so bleak.

Chuck and June putting bead board up in the basement. It will look great—just like you wanted it.

Up at 4 a.m. My brain is in constant motion. I'm starting to put together a collage with photos of you and our boats. Now that basement is put together I have an art center and head full of ideas. I'm embracing my memories and putting them in art form.

Connecting from the other side

Today I had a phone "reading" with a friend of Lois's.
He said he heard from you immediately; he saw you holding two signs that said "keep going".
You said it shouldn't have happened. You miss me and feel closer to me than ever.
You weren't very good about expressing your feelings, but you often looked across the room at me in amazement and wondered how I could do all that I did. He said you had great respect for me. (Wow!!)
We had a deep psychic connection and that's why you are feeling all this so strongly. He said you are grieving too and wished you could reach out and touch me. (I wish that too!) You know what I am doing and you love me.

After that reading, it's as if I don't need to write to you at all. You are watching me and are with me all the time. Nice to know.
And I'll keep writing because it feels good.

****

Phone call............... You called me this morning!
I was in the bathroom finishing my makeup when my phone rang. I casually glanced at it and froze. It was your number on the caller ID. I answered with my hand and voice shaking.
Hello???? The voice on the other end said...get this..."I'm returning your call, I see I missed a call from you." It was a woman who I don't know saying she had two missed calls from my number. She is new in town and has been assigned your old phone number. Our phones have been communicating! Lois told me to keep your phone plugged in from now on! I will...........Call again, please!!!

Memory

I remember a picnic…..
We had a basket with cheese and wine to share.
You were wearing black pants,
white shirt and loafers.
Geez, it was a picnic
and you were dressed
for going to the bank!
I loved that about you---
always wanting to look good.
And, oh, you did---so very, very good.

Alone

Alone in the dark of night
I sit under the starry sky.
Memories float by,
A slide show in my mind.
Missing you is filled
With pain.
The weight of it
Is heavy on my heart.
And yet, I smile
As you smile back at me.

December

Reading "Alone in the Kitchen with an Eggplant". Ann Patchett is talking about living alone. I don't mind being alone, at all. I do mind that you're not here. There's a difference!

****

Marilyn has finished her Larry piece. It's fabulous. I'm taking it to CT with me so my family can see it. I'll have it framed when I get back. And, I'm bringing my scrapbook (memory book) with me too.

****

Well, it's finished. My first collage featuring you. It's a combination of water color, photographs and some raffia (to resemble grass). I'm calling it "A Man and Three Boats"

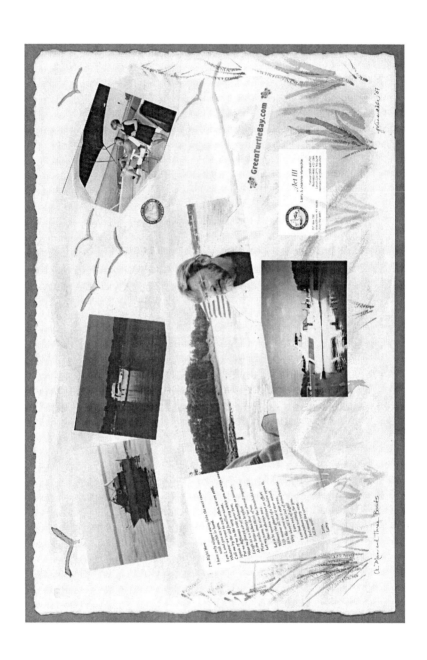

Christmas in Connecticut

Our first Christmas without you. How will we handle our grief together? You will be so missed.

Dad is sick again. Nursing home is discouraging visitors. There is a highly contagious flu going around.

Russ made chili and said he missed his buddy sitting at the bar watching him. I though I heard you laugh from your seat at the bar this morning—you always enjoyed watching our crazy antics.

Dad ended up in ER again. We visited him back at the nursing home for what was to have been our Christmas eve dinner with him. Very weak and confused. He won't be with us for Christmas dinner.

Margie made her traditional potato salad without you as her sous-chef. She missed you. Andy joined us and we all gave him a hard time while I was making chicken roll-ups for dinner. Margie said "Larry would have loved this afternoon." We all sipped Famous Grouse. (Russ and I had each bought a bottle for a toast to you.)

Russ made a fabulous dinner, we watched "It's a Wonderful Life". I went upstairs to take my contacts out and suddenly lost it. I sobbed my little self to sleep. I miss you so….I love you!!

Christmas morning included a few tears….I gave the coin purses made with your fabrics.

I put one of your monogrammed brass buttons in each one and sprayed your Givenchy Gentleman inside. Kate sobbed and said it smelled like you. Laurie told us she had gone to a reading where you came through to say what a great job Russ was doing taking care of me. Yes, he is!

****

Christmas coin purses

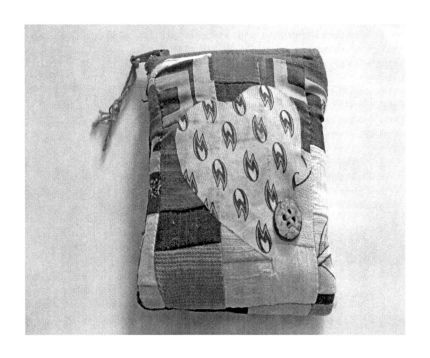

Another of Russ's great dinners. Dad was able to join us. We all went to bed early with a gentle snow falling and me cuddling your black sweater...I want to cuddle you!! What will my life be like from now on???

Later.......

The mouse!

I woke up to a mouse sitting on your blue oxford cloth shirt that I've been wearing. He was looking right at me! Think Stuart Little. I went to get Russ and when we looked back in the bedroom the mouse was perched on the rim of the glass that was on the bedside table. He was drinking my scotch!! Russ got him easily, we think he was drunk! We all said it was a visit from Larry!! You wanted to be with us or was it the lure of the scotch!!??

****

New Year's Eve Day

Dad is getting better. We are actually taking him to the cousins' breakfast on Saturday. The same breakfast that was to be the last time they all saw you a year ago. You said goodbye and picked up the tab. They all remember that—a treasured memory.

Happy New Year! HA!

Will it be happy? What am I looking forward to? I can't even imagine what this next year will be like. I'm going to try to do more art work, sell more houses, not cry so much and get your office converted to my space—make it into a girlie room. So there!!

Spending New Year's Eve with Maryann was the right thing to do. She is so supportive in a non-intrusive way. It was good for me to see how she has put her life together---alone in a new town.

****

Oh, what a month lies ahead. **The dreaded month of January**. What will I do on the 19th besides light candles and cry? Oh baby, oh baby...........

****

I'm going to have a gathering here on the 19th. I will display Marilyn's Larry piece.
We named it "I'm Right Here" I'm having it framed and I'm even making a flyer to tell about the piece. We'll have cocktails and hors d' oeuvres. Our friends are wonderful!

I picked up the piece today. It is fabulous! Kathy came over to see it and had a glass of wine. She has been my rock!

What a year this has been for me-------sad, angry, frightened, devastated, pissed, sad, sometimes hysterical, and always treasuring your love and our memories. Thank you for those.

The first year is over. Why don't I feel better? I thought "they" said just get through the first year. Well, I'm through it and it doesn't feel better.

****

You lied to me who told me time would ease my pain"
Edna St. Vincent Millay

****

I'm Right Here

The Day

Friends filled our house. My book club (both of them!) friends, the Mettler Mavens, and of course, our dear friends who truly share my loss all came together to honor you. While we shed a few tears, we shared laughter, memories and love. And lots of good food and drink.

Pat said she still wants to "bop you over the head" for leaving us. I often feel that way too. I told someone that if you walked in the door I would have to decide whether to kiss you or slap you!

The house was filled with good Karma—I know you were watching and enjoying the scene. Oh, how my heart still aches for you.

The Next Day......

Today feels like such a let down. Last night was filled with laughter, friends, love and memories embraced. Today, it's emptiness and sadness.

THE TRUTH

Friends who truly care,
Family is always there.
And, remember this
At the end of day,
You are on your own,
You are alone.

****

A Year Ago.....

A year ago today we were planning your Celebration of Life. This was the day Russ, Laurie, Margie and I went to Kennedy's to plan the menu. I can always feel their love around me. They loved you too.

I miss you, I miss you, I miss you. I will always love you!

Still January....

Tonight I read though all the sympathy cards again. There are so many and with passages so true for you.

A Life Well-lived
Is a legacy
Of joy and pride and pleasure,
A loving, lasting memory
Our grateful hearts will treasure.

****

Nothing is ever
wholly lost.
That which is
Excellent
remains forever
a part of
this universe.

How appropriate these verses are with the presentation of the Larry Vansickle Memorial Award scheduled for next week. You have left a legacy and I am so proud of you. Russ and Laurie have agreed to fly out to attend the ceremony with me.

****

January 29

What an honor was bestowed on you today. Cal spoke of all you had done for the organization and the industry. He spoke of the long and enduring friendship you two shared and how much he missed you. When Randy accepted the award, he said "I would not be where I am today without Larry." The award recognizes your ability to work cooperatively with competitors and regulators. You were always the diplomat.

This award will carry on your legacy for years to come.

A group of us gathered later for dinner and toasted and roasted you! We shed tears and laughed a lot too. You were an icon to many.

I worry that I didn't show you enough that I loved you so. You made my life so wonderful. Did I appreciate enough your kind, gentle ways, your support of me in anything I wanted to do. I thought you were so smart. Please let me know that you knew I adored you and nearly worshipped you.

****

Russ and Laurie (Margie too) took some of your sweaters when they left. You had so many. I wear them often. Oh fine….bring on the tears!!!

****

If tears are a shower for the soul, then
mine should be squeaky clean!

****

March

Tonight I was in County Market sneaking a handful of sesame sticks from the bulk food bin. I thought about how you would never have done that---*stealing* food from County Market!! You were so honest!

Are you that cardinal who sits in the top of the pear tree right outside of the bedroom window each morning?? I hope so…………..

April

Last night I dreamed a man was holding me. Not you, but Paul Newman! And then someone else…not you. It felt so good, so comforting. I remember asking "him" if I could just stay there for awhile because it felt so good.

I walked to your tree this morning. There it was------your name, the dates and my inscription. "Love Always". And, you're not there. Where the hell are you??

****

Seems like every day I write, "I miss you", "I love you". I know I sound like a broken record! Sorry about that--I can't help it!

I lay
   In my morning bed
   without you.
Breakfast, lunch
   and dinner,
   You are not here.

I sip my scotch
   without you.

Eating, drinking, sleeping
   you are not here.
I lay in my nighttime bed
   without you.

I wake, I play, I sing,
   I dance.
Without you.

May

Guess what I did today!? I got a kitten! I named her Lulu in honor of you. Lulu Marie, her initials are the same as yours! (LMV)

This morning I woke up and she was peeing on my leg! Oh well, time to change to the spring linens anyway.

Lulu is so entertaining, I've hardly cried this week. Not to worry; I can do it at the drop of a hat!

Tonight we are having severe storms. We would be up watching the weather, sipping scotch and enjoying being together. We were so good at that!

Working in the yard today and sobbing my little heart out. Everything looks so good. You would be so proud and you made it all happen. And, now I get to do all the work! The other night someone said "your yard looks like a park". What a compliment to all your efforts. Will I be able to maintain it? Another thing to worry about!

June

Six goldfinch in the feeder right now! And, now eight!

Making iced tea and remembering how there were always two pitchers in the fridge. Regular for me and green for you. You drank all that damn green tea and you still died!

Sometimes when I'm sitting here reading or watching T.V. , I think "oh, Larry should be calling soon." I'm still waiting to hear from you.

****

Two more days until what would have been our 41st anniversary. I so knew I was doing the right thing on our wedding day. I'm remembering how we used to sit up talking about religion, politics, current events, our dreams We liked the same television shows---mostly. Sorry I never got into StarTrek. You liked the movies that I liked. You weren't afraid to show your feminine side. You liked my girlfriends and they liked you. The other day, Allison said, "Larry was everybody's friend".

****

Recently, when showing a house. I saw a saying on the wall that said: *The first moment I beheld him, my heart was irrevocably gone. (jane austen)* My heart is still irrevocably gone!

****

Laurie has made an appointment for me with a "reader" next week when I'm at the cottage. I'm excited about that! Hope to hear from you!!

June 24....41 years ago we walked down the aisle into our wonderful life together. You are supposed to be here with me drinking our morning coffee and planning our anniversary dinner. I bought you a card, but where to send it? No address---where the hell are you??

O.k., so here's what I did on our anniversary:
I had a manicure,
a pedicure,
a facial,
and a brow, lip and bikini wax.
$300.00 and happy anniversary to me!
So there!

At the cottage.

I so love it here. You did too. This is where we were going to spend our retirement.

So many thoughts this morning.........this is my place of peace and comfort. Yes, it feels so different without you, knowing that you won't be here to plan the remodeling and enjoy more time here. You loved it here. I believe we were both at peace here.

Russ fixed one of our classic cottage meals—his signature fish on the grill along with sausage, peppers and onions, sautéed squash and roasted potatoes. We toasted you as we always do.

****

Today I did all the little errands we always did on our spring visit here---alone. Bought cleaning supplies, groceries, a new rug for the back porch, some new lamps, chairs for the backyard, flowers for the garden pots—all without you! Damnit!!

****

"The Voice of the Sea speaks to the Soul"
Kate Chopin

****

July 1st

My reading with the psychic, Laura.

Wow! She knew lots about me and us. So much to process.
She said you were there and talking in her ear telling her about my
using your putter in the recent golf outing. She said she was seeing
pink. Yes! It was a Rally for Life outing for breast cancer! She said
you loved me so much and admired me too and how much our time
together had meant to you. It was a comforting experience.
I was pretty skeptical. I'll go back again with a more open mind.
Thanks for being there with me.

The next day

I dreamed last night that a man was telling me to get busy with my
writing. In my session with Laura yesterday, you told her I should
do more painting and that I had more creative ability than I gave
myself credit for. I guess I'd better get to it!

Lulu is such a comfort to me. This morning she snuggled up to
my face and curled up beside me. That's why I slept so good. Now
enjoying the beautiful morning and missing you....as always.

****

Dad fell last night and cracked his head open. He is a mess. Poor guy!

Saw Dad—he is doing o.k. He has stitches, a patch over one eye and the other is bruised. He said there was lots of blood and it scared him. His whole situation just breaks my heart.

****

Tomorrow I leave here. I wish I could stay forever. But…here I have no social life, all my friends are in Illinois. I missed several parties while I was gone, no girlfriends here to share a glass of wine. I would be here alone: writing, painting, drinking too much wine (I already do that!). It would be me and Lulu. I know friends would visit and you wouldn't be here. Of course, my dear family would be nearby. Would they feel obligated to be with me? Would I be a burden? I truly don't know what to do!

Kate and Sara are here tonight. They made eggplant parmesan for dinner—delicious! I was sautéing some onions and Sara said, "You cook? I didn't know that because Larry always did the cooking." Everyone misses you.

****

****

Will I ever sleep in the middle of the bed? Live in a different house?
Have sex with another man? (Yuck!) Let another man see me
naked? (Yikes!) Do I even want to do any of these things? I don't
know. I wonder...............

****

Home again

It seems I cry much less now. And, the hole in my heart is still there—full of sadness and yearning.

Today I had to replace the light bulbs in my closet. That required a big ladder that I had to maneuver up the stairs. I've never had to do that before. Another first---thanks a lot!!

****

July 19th

A year and half ago you left me. I cried in the shower this morning. You were the only person in the whole world to whom I could tell anything and say whatever was on my mind. I always knew your love was unconditional.

A little pity party going on here this weekend. You would be so proud! More crying. I just feel so empty. What I am supposed to do and why?? It all seems so meaningless without you to share stories, insights, opinions---yours and mine. I need to hear your thoughts, ideas, and I miss your compliments. I have to tell myself how good I look and how clever I am. I feel confused, at sea and without focus.

****

Another dream last night

I was talking to you on the phone. I heard your voice and your laugh.
I said something about being lonely, missing hugs and sex. You said,
"I'll work on it"
I said, "Oh yeah sure. What can you do from where you are?" You
replied, "I can get things done from here." It was strange, but I was
really talking to you! It was your voice!!!

****

Just saw this quote: "Trust the Journey".......I'm trying!

August

Here's the truth: I still can't park in the middle of the garage. I still
stack pillows on your side of the bed as if there's a body there. Your
clothes are still in the closet.
Yet, I cleaned out your bathroom and sold your car. Go figure!

****

I'm meeting the girls for coffee this morning. Then, work in the
yard, but I have no plans for tonight. I was busy every night during
the week and then, nothing on Saturday night. I hate being home
by myself on Saturday night. We always had plans, always together
on Saturday night.

Next morning

I survived! Sold a house last night and didn't get home until after 8 o'clock.

Tricia called today and walked down memory lane. We laughed our heads off remembering our good times together. It felt good to laugh so much. Of course, we shed a few tears too.

I'm taking an art class in mixed media at Parkland. I'm hoping to use the fabric pieces I have left over from the piece Marilyn did. Now that the basement is all cleaned up and organized, thanks to Chuck and June, I have set up a studio of sorts. It feels very therapeutic, as though you are there with me. Scott hooked up the cable for the old t.v. down there . I can watch the Food Channel or Golden Girls reruns while I'm working. I usually have a glass of wine or a cup of tea.
Sometimes the tears drop by for a visit. And, always the memories are there keeping me company.

****

I just looked at the photo of you that I keep in the back of this journal. It always makes my heart stop and the tears spring up.

****

There has to be light at the end of this dark tunnel!!

****

Musings

I continue to wonder if you were thinking of me in your last moments. When you stopped breathing, did my face flash before you? Were you thinking of me that last day? I can't stop thinking about this!

****

Thinking back, I never really had marriage in my plans for the future. Mainly because I'd never been popular with the boys and I saw so many unhappy, dull marriages. I would be independent; travel and enjoy the single life. Then you came into my life—I fought it for a long time. I didn't want to marry. Especially a guy without a college education from a small town in ILLINOIS!!
I did not want to be a Midwesterner . I had envisioned the city life. I used to say that there were two things I knew for certain—the sun sets in the west and I will never live in Illinois! Well.........you kept at it. You kept kissing me! That damn kiss, that voice and that teddy bear hug of yours. Wrapped in your arms was heaven to me.

****

You would be so pissed by what is going on with the republicans. They have demonstrated themselves to be the hypocrites that they are. I wish you were here to share your perspective. You always had such insight.

****

I want to travel, create art, take photos, be with family and friends.
Cry when I want to and I want to right now!!

****

I was thinking will I ever get over you and realized I don't want to!
I think I will make you the focus of my art work!
Good idea! Brilliant, in fact!!!

****

The Kiss of Life

He was wearing a
Blue oxford cloth shirt,
Gray slacks and black loafers—
Soft blond hair, blue eyes, too.

He took my hand in his
'Come, help me with these
Damn ice cube trays.'
How could I know that request
Would make me his wife?

Our friends insisted
That we meet.
I did not know what to do
About love.
My plan to avoid it—
Career and travel to exotic places,
The independent single life for me.

His lips touched mine
In the kitchen that night,
It was a fateful moment.
My head screamed no, no, no!
My heart cried yes, yes, yes!

It was the kiss
That changed my life.

September

I'm reading a book that has captured my heart......<u>The Cure for Anything is Salt Water</u>, *How I Threw My Life Overboard and Found Happiness at Sea* written by a woman.
This speaks to my search for "what should I do with my life now that you are gone".

****

Had an orgasmic dream last night. I felt it down to my toes. Just me and the orgasm and it felt good. Sorry you weren't there!

****

Tonight dinner with Marilyn and Don. I had a Jeannie Martini--- a scotch martini. They make them especially for me at Sunsinger. We talked a lot about you—Marilyn was a fan.
Now I'm home feeling sad and missing you. You were such a presence, a force in my life. I miss you so.

****

I made reservations to fly to Seattle for Thanksgiving with Diane. I need to start making my own traditions. More baby steps.

****

My mind is churning with ideas for a large collage piece of you and about you.

I have so many ideas. I wish I could just work on art projects. Create instead of selling real estate!!!

****

Sat. morning----good sleep last night. Just before waking we had a kiss---nice dream.

Would that it were real! Another day ahead...................

****

Scotch and Soda

October

Watching TV. I keep seeing Viagra and Cialas commercials. I could just scream..in fact, I just did! They keep improving them! And too late for us. Damn you!!

****

Obama is president-elect!! When it was announced I burst into tears! You should be here to share this momentous occasion. I'm so excited and so sad. Tears of joy and sadness. Missing you…. There's a hole in my heart.

****

Watching Ghost Whisperer, one of your favorite shows. I wish you could tell me about crossing over.

****

I'm working on another art piece. I don't know if it's any good. It's all about you and it's very therapeutic. Art therapy for the soul—mine!

****

Golf today with Tom and Joan. I had some good drives and few awesome putts. Thanks to your putter!

****

Watching CBS Sunday morning, reading the paper with coffee and a fire and baking bread too. All **without you!!!!** What am I to do????

****

November

Thanksgiving in Seattle. A new experience for me. It's beautiful here.

Diane's decorating had inspired me to change your bathroom at home. From yours to a cool guest bath. I'm going to make it girlie, whimsical. It's a step---maybe my first---in my healing process. It will take more—that hole in my heart is very large.

Fun shopping with Diane. I bought more art supplies and an iPod. More progress.

Trip home was a nightmare. I kept thinking that you would have hated the four hour delay sitting in the airport. Home after midnight!

December

Girls night here. I made a yummy dinner, if do say so myself. Chicken picatta, rice pilaf, my signature salad and your roasted green beans. We had such a good time—these are wonderful women!

In Connecticut

A wild wonderful snow storm ---New England at its best!

Visited Dad today at the nursing home. What a depressing place to be. It's so sad.
This is when I know you did it the right way---in spite of all the pain it has caused me. I cannot imagine you in such a place and me having to visit you there.

****

Christmas Eve—We all shed tears for you. Margie gave us little notecards that she had made. Mine had a quote from Helen Keller: *"What you have loved and enjoyed deeply you can never lose, for all that you love deeply becomes part of you."* So true!

Christmas morning---Our usual gift mix-up always makes us laugh and think about Mom. Russ was totally blown away by his big surprise gift, our trip to Hilton Head for his birthday in April. Kate made a set of clues and your picture was part of one of the clues and she burst into tears when she saw the picture. Tears all around again. I love you!!

****

Cousins' Day....the tradition continues. We had our day-after-Christmas lunch and shopping trip. Lots of laughs. They are wonderful!

****

Dinner at Rudy and Evelyn's. Peggy and Judy said they felt you were with us all evening. Judy said she heard your laugh. You are amazing!!

****

Kate made dinner for us at their condo. Yum—it was such fun seeing her cooking in her Vera Bradley apron. Andy is a dear. I wonder if they will get married. So sorry you never got to meet him. You would like him.

****

Kathy and Maria called and want me to go to Florida with the girls at the end of January. I said I couldn't go—no money, got to work. They said YES! So I guess I'm going. It will be diversion for the second anniversary of your leaving......without notice!!

****

HAPPY NEW YEAR!!! Shit!

We toasted you last night with your favorite, Famous Grouse. Russ, Laurie, Gene, Marie and Me.
We all miss you terribly! I drank too much—so what's new?

****

I found this on a sympathy card: "In the middle of winter, I finally learned that there was an invincible summer." *Albert Camus*
Will I ever learn this??

****

Back home again. It's good to be here in my (our) bed with your pictures, sweaters and memories surrounding me. What will this year bring??

****

I'm reading a book about memoir*. In it she says to write every day,
even if it's just a list.

So here's my list.
What I miss about you:
your voice,
your touch,
your wonderful laugh,
cuddling with you,
seeing you naked in the shower,
your cooking,
the way you would look at me and I'd know how much you loved me,
your insights about people, politics, and history,
our daily phone calls,
the way you took care of me,
listening to you counsel others on the phone.
I miss our closeness more than the sex;
I just want your arms around me and to feel your beard on my face.
I carry your picture with me all the time!

And, just for the record, here's another list!
Things about you that pissed me off:
You smoked.
You drank too much.
You drove too slow.
You wouldn't exercise.
You were terrible with money.
You hated shopping!
(Hmm.....that's not a very long list. See above!)

*The Memoir Project, Marion Roach Smith

Jeannie Vansickle   80

The dreaded month of January

It will soon be two years since you left me. I think I'm still in a daze.

I am a mess! Frustrated with business, worried about $ and the dreadful date is approaching. I dropped a spoon while fixing dinner and I began screaming at you for leaving me in this situation. You bastard!! That's what I said….sorry!
I must get through this week.

1/18
Donna and Margie J. here for a support sleep over. I made shrimp parmesan—a new recipe you never got to experience. They loved it! We toasted you. Donna said what she remembers most about you is your wonderful laugh. Yes, it was wonderful! You were the unseen guest.

Scott brought a white rose in your honor. Mary and Grace stopped by with a candle and a sweet card. It was good to have a diversion during this time. And I'm looking forward to the Florida trip---another diversion. I am, however, really getting worried about money!

****

'

The Day

Two years ago today I was driving your car back to Champaign—screaming, cursing, sobbing, moaning---you were dead! How could it be? How would I survive? The pain still fills my heart every day. Everyone thinks I'm so strong----WRONG!!! There's that hole in my heart.

Our friends came by tonight and we toasted you. (We do that a lot!) So many notes and emails remembering you and supporting me. I watched the DVD and cried my eyes out. I love you!!

****

Count down to Girls Florida Trip!

FLORIDA in January!!!

Oh my god! What a trip. On the 23rd, the anniversary of your celebration of life, we drank a toast to you and then went out to dinner. That night we watched Mama Mia and laughed and danced til the wee hours. We dubbed ourselves the Dancing Queens.

For five days I laughed, danced, shopped, drank wine, ate seafood. And for five days......I did not cry!!!

****

Maybe there is light at the end of this dark tunnel????

****

Out of the Tunnel

Looking back over the past five years, I realize how far I've come on this journey.

That trip to Florida with the Dancing Queens was a major crossroad. We have made many more trips together and continue to share laughter and wine.

I've learned so much about myself. Lord knows, I've read enough books that I should be perfectly enlightened! I know I am a different person from the woman who drove that car back home screaming and cursing. I've reached into the spiritual world (and the spirit world!). I read somewhere that grief never ends, it transforms itself. It has transformed me, as well. My grief has become an agent of change.

Taking the Plunge

In the Spring I decided to try online dating services. It was something I thought I *should* do to move ahead. Here's what I have to say about that experience—Are you kidding me??? I know there are many women and men who have found love and happiness through an online matching service. Hats off to them! My experience was quite different. I mean, really....if you were a man seriously looking for woman would you have your profile picture taken in your undershirt sitting on a lawn chair in your garage? Or, better yuck, in front of your RV holding a very large, very dead fish!! I am obviously am not the woman you are looking for!

I did actually have a couple of connections. The first was a guy, Sam, who preferred older women. After several online exchanges, I called him as he suggested. I pushed the buttons on the phone with deep breaths and trembling fingers. Big gulp!
He had all the plans made to take the train from the east coast to meet me in Chicago (he had no idea that I was actually two hours from Chicago). I asked him for a picture since he had seen mine. He gave me his website and assured me that I would not be disappointed as he was quite good looking. Au contraire!! He was quite unsavory—gnarly and scraggly. When I told him I wasn't interested, he insisted that I give "us" a chance! What us?? He kept calling me and became a phone stalker. I never answered and finally blocked his number. A wacko!

Then there was Henry. He met my criteria: No ex-wife, no children, dead parents, liked wine and good food. He lived in Chicago—not too far away. We had lots of online exchanges. He was going to come to Champaign on a specific date. I had already decided where we would have lunch and planned the day. Then---he disappeared from the site! Gone, never to be heard from again. I have to admit I was looking forward to the adventure of a possible new relationship. After a few more "I love my RV" hits, I left the site. Enough of that for me!

****

April in Paris

Later that Spring I went to Paris with my friend, Diane. When she suggested the trip, my immediate reaction was the usual. "I can't afford it. I have to work."
I remember that I was with Kate when I got the email and she immediately said, "You have to go! Larry would want you to." I knew she was right.

The trip was fabulous! We stayed in an apartment in the 13th Arrondissement . For a week we could pretend we actually lived in Paris. I had breakfast one morning in a sidewalk café near the Mouffatard Market that Hemingway wrote about in the opening chapter of "A Movable Feast"!!

The Art of Healing

I continue to create my mixed media pieces, many still featuring Larry. One of my favorites is a picture of him with a glass of scotch. I used the wrapping paper from a bottle of Glenlevet for the background. There are my signature hearts and gold highlights. I call it "Scotch and Soda". It makes me smile.
There are others that I like too: "A Hole in My Heart", "Til Death Do Us Part", "Little Boy Blue", "Gone", "Walk with Me" and one that features me called "It's Possible to be Both Fabulous and Flawed".

The Cottage

The cottage continues to be a refuge. A place where the memories are alive, the place where we planned to spend our retirement. I've made some improvements and it has felt like a tribute to Larry. We had a vision and I've managed to bring part of it to life. We have a new sunroom replacing the old enclosed porch where Larry always sat with a book and his favorite view of the salt marshes. I have hung his picture in that room where it belongs. Maybe I belong there too.

Travel

Traveling was another great diversion for me. Besides Paris, there have been numerous trips to Florida, Hilton Head for Russ's 60th, Thanksgivings in Seattle and Albuquerque and many fun filled weekends in Chicago. And, always Christmas in Connecticut. Not to mention the Grief Coach Academy events in California.
Next year: Italy!

Reflections

I often think about our rash decision to go live on our boat. It impacted greatly on our (and now my) financial situation and, at the same time, it was the best decision we ever made. If we had waited for retirement to do it, it never would have happened! Those five years were some of the best of our time together. We made wonderful friends and the bond between the two of us was strengthened immeasurably.

****

I heard this on a TED talk: …when you're faced with something that's unexpected, unwanted and uncertain, consider that it just may be a gift. Should I consider Larry's death a gift? The gift of grief, hmmm………..

****

Another thought: Grief is not about recovery or healing. It's learning to live without someone while still embracing life.

****

I don't know what lies ahead as this journey continues. And, I'm excited about the possibilities and opportunities in my future. All I know right now is that I thought I couldn't have a life without him and now I know I can.

And....I still sleep on my side of the bed and last week I parked my car in the middle of the garage for the first time!

****

Happiness is a choice......I choose it!

"I walked a mile with pleasure,
She chatted all the way.
But left me none the wiser
for all she had to say.

I walked a mile with sorrow
and ne'er a word said she.
But, oh, the things I learned from her,
when sorrow walked with me."

From *The Best Loved Poems of the American People*

Acknowledgements

First, I must thank my wonderful little family for their unwavering love and support:

My brother, Russ who was totally there for me along the way. He became the caretaker of Larry's ashes and distributed them "everywhere". My sister-in-law, Laurie who shared so many tears and glasses of wine as we waded through our grief. Kate, the wonder niece, who told me she considered Larry her second father and in tough situations often thinks "what would Larry want me to do?" And, of course, my dear sister, Margie who loved Larry like another brother, ignored his vices and valued the goodness in him. She shared my sorrow and rejoiced in my healing.

Our dear friends who were my rocks: Tom and Joan who were willing to be a threesome on the golf course and for so many lunches and dinners too. Scott and Marian who hosted me for many Sunday night dinners and kept Larry's memory alive. The five of us became The White Jacket Dinner Club in his honor.

And, what would I have done without my Dancing Queens (Kathy, Maria, Kelly, Terri, Deb and Mary)? They literally saved me from the depths. First, insisting that I make that trip to Florida on the second anniversary of losing Larry. And then, becoming my "always there" support group and making me laugh even when I wanted to cry.

All the wonderful friends who cared so much: Jim and Sandy, who gave me refuge in Florida, Marilyn, who honored Larry with her art, Pat and Norm, Ronna and Tim, Lori and Reese, Teri, Joni and Allison. Oh, and Carla who endured all my sadness and just listened while doing my nails. Iris and Dick who have eased my financial worries with their loving commitment and expertise.

Chuck and June who became my "go to" buddies for support and all things domestic. They made over my garage, cleaned out my basement, supervised yard work and handled numerous repairs. Not to mention, being there for emergency phone calls! I am ever so grateful! And, of course, my dear Diane who dragged me off to Paris! Jan and Bev, who knew Larry before I did, and shared many memories and lunches with me. Sid & Kathy and Steve & Maria who have so generously made me a part of their families.

All my cousins who gave me comfort and support. Lois, who helped me connect with "the other side".

My Keller Williams family who offered a safe place when staying home was not a good idea. Especially, Sharon who put up with a weeping roommate at that real estate convention less than a month after Larry died.

My Life Coach, Sherry Hill, whose guidance led me to the Grief Coach Academy where I found inspiration from a new community of friends and a new purpose for my life. They are all just a phone call away for love and support.

I'll always be grateful that Larry was with his dear friends when he took his last breath. Thank you, Cal and Val and Jeff.

To those who I forgot to mention............thanks for everything! Lucky me!

Special Thanks

A special thank you to my friends at the law offices of Nally, Bauer, Feinen and Mann for donating the tree that was planted in Larry's memory. I will be forever grateful for your generosity and compassion.

Thank you, Dory O'Toole for making my memory book a much classier tribute. Larry deserved more that the three ring binder I was using until you came along.

And, thank you, Kate Lund for your editorial assistance and review. You are the best!!

Recommended Reading

Helpful Resources

We Are Their Heaven, Allison Du Bois

Widow to Widow, Genevieve Davis Ginsburg, M.S

As We Grieve, Jan Groft

*Living When A Loved One Has Died, Earl A. Grollman

Sorry for Your Loss: What People Who Are Grieving WishYou Knew, Alicia King

Getting Back to Life When Grief Won't Heal, Phyllis Kosminsky, Ph.D

Broken Open, Elizabeth Lessor

I Wasn't Ready to Say Goodbye, Brook Noel & Pamela D. Blair

Healing a Spouse's Grieving Heart, Alan Wolfelt

Memoirs

The Year of Magical Thinking, Joan Didion

Comfort: A Journey Through Grief, Ann Hood

Epilogue, Ann Roiphe

Making Toast, Roger Rosenblatt

Signs of Life, Natalie Taylor

From Heartbreak to Happiness, Aurora Winter

About the Author

Jeannie Vansickle has a Master's degree in Educational Psychology. She has experience as an educator, administrator, trainer and speaker.

She developed and taught a course "Writing Down the Memories" for seniors at Parkland College.

She is the author of "Lizzie's Legacy", a collection of family recipes and memories.

Jeannie lives in Champaign, Illinois with her naughty cat, Lulu. She spends as much time as she can at her cottage at the Connecticut shore. Lulu gets to go too.

She enjoys reading, writing , creating art, cooking, entertaining and traveling while attempting to keep up with the yard work. In addition, she is dedicated to coaching women who are struggling with the loss of a spouse.

Jeannie is a certified "From Heartbreak to Happiness" grief coach.

Visit her at www.heartfeltcoach.com where you can view more of her art pieces and learn about her coaching and her availability as a speaker.

CPSIA information can be obtained at www.ICGtesting.com
Printed in the USA
LVOW080157151212

311733LV00002B/4/P